CLOSE ESCAPES

ALSO BY STEPHEN KUUSISTO

POETRY

Old Horse, What Is to Be Done?

Letters to Borges

Only Bread, Only Light

MEMOIR

Have Dog, Will Travel: A Poet's Journey

Eavesdropping: A Memoir of Blindness and Listening

Planet of the Blind

NONFICTION

Do Not Interrupt: A Playful Take on the Art of Conversation

The Poet's Notebook (editor, with Deborah Tall and David Weiss)

CLOSE ESCAPES
Stephen Kuusisto

COPPER CANYON PRESS
PORT TOWNSEND, WASHINGTON

Copyright 2025 by Stephen Kuusisto
All rights reserved
Printed in the United States of America

Cover art: Ulriche Jantjes, *In the Still of the Night,* 2024. Oil on canvas, 91 × 76 cm. Photo by Mia Thom.

Copper Canyon Press is in residence at Fort Worden State Park in Port Townsend, Washington, under the auspices of Centrum. Centrum is a gathering place for artists and creative thinkers from around the world, students of all ages and backgrounds, and audiences seeking extraordinary cultural enrichment.

LIBRARY OF CONGRESS CATALOGING-IN-PUBLICATION DATA
Names: Kuusisto, Stephen, author.
Title: Close escapes / Stephen Kuusisto.
Description: Port Townsend, Washington : Copper Canyon Press, 2025. | Summary: "A collection of poems by Stephen Kuusisto"— Provided by publisher.
Identifiers: LCCN 2024052763 (print) | LCCN 2024052764 (ebook) | ISBN 9781556596896 (paperback) | ISBN 9781619323001 (epub)
Subjects: LCGFT: Poetry.
Classification: LCC PS3561.U85 C58 2025 (print) | LCC PS3561.U85 (ebook) | DDC 811/.54—dc23/eng/20241121
LC record available at https://lccn.loc.gov/2024052763
LC ebook record available at https://lccn.loc.gov/2024052764

COPPER CANYON PRESS
Post Office Box 271
Port Townsend, Washington 98368
www.coppercanyonpress.org

ACKNOWLEDGMENTS

Some of these poems have appeared, often in different forms, in *Orion Magazine, Red Wheelbarrow, Nine Mile Magazine,* and on the poetry pages of the Academy of American Poets' Poem-a-Day.

For Jim Crenner

CONTENTS

    3   I was alone in a room with a radio

THE COLLAPSE OF A WISH

    7   How does it begin

    8   A repeated fury has me by the toe

    9   The day was like a forest of stone with stringent ballads

    10   Topographers of the eighteenth century

    11   My louche

    12   Dear Id: I have just now stepped off the train

    13   I bought an umbrella from a street vendor

    14   I spent a long winter reading Edith Södergran

    15   There was this Russian place in Helsinki

    16   I wonder whether I can stick to one thought

    17   I went to the river to find my old Moses basket

    18   I loved my mother

    19   Wittgenstein says our visual field has no limits

    20   He sees at last infirmity is a trick

    21   Like a falling leaf

    22   The blind kid

DARK JOYS

25 Picking mushrooms in rain
26 Pressed flower I found
27 Alone in the attic with a gramophone and comic books
28 I'm the blind kid again
29 Ghosts
30 I'm working my magic outside a sad hotel
31 I write: "if I could command you"
32 Helsinki 1980
33 Poets in America disappear while still alive
34 Now he's getting old he wants Bach
35 Open your eyes
36 I used to go to the botanical gardens in Helsinki
37 Frail wisdom
38 The paper wasps flew all afternoon through the ruined woodpile
39 Old baseball glove
40 In the monastery at Valamo
41 He spends his life
42 I love the horse at Lascaux
43 Write poems in the mornings

TOUCH IT

- 47 I fill my bag with apples
- 48 Please Lord don't let me die in this bitterness
- 49 I know what they did
- 50 Haavikko says
- 51 You saw the sightless men of Paris
- 52 When you're blind but can still
- 53 Late afternoon
- 54 So much of what I do
- 55 Reading Nietzsche
- 56 Sometimes I feel like Rousseau
- 57 The branches
- 58 You know how it is
- 59 I was too blind for the army
- 60 Have you seen the black geese
- 61 Meanwhile   crossing the street

NORDIC ZEN

- 65 In Nordic Zen things simply disappear
- 66 My great-grandfather built
- 67 I drag the old boat to the lakeshore
- 68 No one calls your name quite like the birches

69	Deep down there's moonlight on the river
70	They took us to cemeteries
71	It wasn't much
72	Deep in the night everyone's alive
73	What do the people say in the next village
74	Once on a train to Lapland
75	They used to hang the bread from rafters
76	Death comes so softly
77	Yesterday I climbed into a boat

HOMINATICUM

81	As a child I harvested
82	Happily sharing our sanity
83	The wall clock says no one checks out alive
84	Sometimes a poem is a way of
85	Big poem mates with little poem
86	I watch you sewing
87	You touch my hair
88	Cold river of childhood
89	Growing old talking to myself
90	Meanwhile
91	*A dear child has many names*
92	I am

93	Some children knew the names of birds
94	*When spirits come in the forest*
95	You bend to the pavement
96	Seeing I was blind and on vacation
97	I dreamed last night of a friend whom I insulted
98	In another dream
99	Winter with a book
100	Now that the wind has stopped
101	One makes the world while drinking tea
102	And slow life is the work

EMPTY PLACES

105	Every morning the wisdom of trees
106	It's raining
107	In the airport where women and men
108	They set the boy
109	Oh Hush Puppies
110	Oh Wallace Stevens
111	Oh Muriel Rukeyser
112	Oh Auden
113	Oh Pentti
114	Oh Caruso
115	I'm reading the youthful notebooks

116	I love it whenever the poets say angels visit them
117	A poem a day
118	Coffee late morning
119	*ABOUT THE AUTHOR*

CLOSE ESCAPES

~

I was alone in a room with a radio   a dog   and a glass of water
There was a chair   a bed   the usual hotel furnishings
My connecting flight had been canceled   and it was toward midnight
The hotel was in a run-down part of the city
I had to take the dog out   I put on her leather harness
Me?   I was wearing track shoes and a rumpled business suit
Out we went   first into a hallway that smelled of soap flakes
Then up to street level   then down a corridor filled with plastic ferns
Until we reached a parking lot
The only place to take the dog   or so I'd been told
And there we were   standing in the nowhere of blindness—
That beautiful nothing with its hope and autonomy and its private song
Shared between man and animal   the oldest song on Earth

THE COLLAPSE OF A WISH

I was born like a forest spirit
Free but endangered, light
And full of forgotten pleasure . . .

EEVA KILPI

~

How does it begin   the collapse of a wish
When you can't ask how it ends
This is a joke of the rich
Who play chess with civic statues

Three crows on my lawn
All dance sideways
Pecking at the remains
Of a Christmas wreath . . .

When I was a lad   well   you know—
I lived in the warrens of an outlawed sect called "the blind"

A repeated fury has me by the toe
You see   the wind from dawn's hourglass
Opened my eyes   and I wasn't ready
Now I want to tear the wreaths off
My neighbor's doors   but it isn't Christmas

So many unknown forces in the genes
Today I am a rabid king
Beware lest I appear on your doorstep
As Pablo Neruda once said   *Please*
I beg a sage tell me   where I can live in peace

~

The day was like a forest of stone with stringent ballads
Some sang the songs   some did not
Most tried to navigate between lithic trees

I have been in more than one ossuary on my travels
Skulls lined up like nouns for schoolchildren
Don't look at me ironically with your postmodern peepers

The falling we will do ere long will be without end

Night and far to go
Wishful songs   some from boyhood
The one about the fish and the old man
The one about rowing and night and far to go
The uproar of living by day and dreaming by night

Your teeth wear out
The brass buttons on Father's uniform glitter up in the attic
And night and far to go
Have I ever told you   my dear   that a succession of
Immense birds guides all my thinking?

~

Topographers of the eighteenth century
Here's snow with its murmuring rhymes and half words
I know how you put this on your maps
Because I also try to avoid temporal distractions

~

My louche   unbuttoned   acerbic   freewheeling side
Pops up all the time   Says what it wants
Says what it wants   Said once
The enemy's stars are the same as ours
Said it to a military recruiter and why not?
And said it once to a government agent
Who was photographing a protest against
Ronald Reagan's suppression of freedom in El Salvador
You know there are honest jobs
Ones where you can make humble and lasting discoveries
And he   of course   photographed me

Dear Id: I have just now stepped off the train
I have raised the flag of metaphor
Beside the painful river of waking
I am standing in tall weeds

At the outer limits of phenomenology
There's a terrible freedom
I am wearing my soulful little eyeglass frames

As I grow older   my hands open more slowly
What is empty turns its face to us
Said Tranströmer long ago
My left hand agrees   longs to touch her

~

I bought an umbrella from a street vendor
The sky was clear
The weather report called for many days of sun
Sometimes you need a prop for the dark
Unconscious side of life

I bought the thing for my dead mother
And then she was there with me on Eighth Street
And the crowd around us formed a dense black ant pile
The confusion all about us was indescribable

∼

I spent a long winter reading Edith Södergran
Alone in the far north—Helsinki

One night   the moon at my window
Reached in and picked my pockets

My great-grandfather was a wheelwright
Hammering slats for infant coffins
In the farther north   He didn't read Baudelaire

Insatiable labor in the age of epidemics
Landscapes in faces
Songs that begin slowly

People die so easily
Many in the early morning

In me is this eye   this stream   this wind
Exactly the number of birds in flight

There was this Russian place in Helsinki
Where the waiter wanted me to order bear

And the taverna on Paros
Where I watched sunlight in a glass of water

Nothing is quite right when you dine alone
But you solve the crossword while also appraising your hands

I wonder whether I can stick to one thought
Like a small hunting dog
Riding the train to New York
Looking at the spoiled factory towns   the haunted river

Can I hold on to a single thought?
I think I can be allowed a murmur
There has to be music in human silence
Shadows fall together in the tall grass of a railroad siding

After this   there may be music
Night crosses the desert of my understanding
I wonder whether I can stick to just one thought
Like the smallest of hunting dogs

I went to the river to find my old Moses basket
Went to the river to scoop up mirror neurons
Went to the river to talk to an old donkey
Now and then I whisper to myself
As if the train station is a library

I loved my mother
She was such a dark person
I see her everywhere in the woods

Wittgenstein says our visual field has no limits
You can see why a blind person admires this
The trick is to live it

Early
Wittgenstein for breakfast
Calling my dog

When a horse passes us
I feel his mystery
Evening sky

He sees at last infirmity is a trick
Something achieved with string

A game best played on the floor—
Puzzle   wish   fear   and ache

Are what a magician is for
It's raining as always

But he has a stick
And he waves it at the orient wind

Like a falling leaf
The boy
How to take him with me
As the years advance

I hear a happy tale   it makes me sad:
No-one will remember me for long
Paavo Haavikko writes

~

The blind kid:
He was never "in" time
Like those oaks you see
In certain forests
Still green
Although we're long into December

DARK JOYS

In memory of Pentti Saarikoski

> *Glorious to be away from the mill at last!*
> *On such a day the sky looks strangely poetic*
> *With all the sad poetry of chimney and of gable.*
>
> DONALD JUSTICE, "SONYA SITS AT THE PIANO, PRACTICING"

Picking mushrooms in rain   laughing—
Slow clumsy man
Dark boot prints
Ancestors behind ferns

I've a magpie for counsel
Something's coming
A hymn in mind
On a long trembling bridge

Yes we fall backward
Into the emptying self
Yes I did want to go somewhere
In the slyness of good faith

Pressed flower I found
A spark of hope
In a long-ago
Finnish Bible
My father carried
Across the Pacific
Then put aside

Sea hibiscus blooms
For only one day
Then smells like carrion

Alone in the attic with a gramophone and comic books
Happy birthday   Son

Far below   the angry parents accuse each other
Of what they'll never become

I'm the blind kid again
Touching a spider's web
She runs to her corner
I press my finger there

Ghosts
In the grass at dusk
Silly he thinks
A cricket animism
No one to tell
But himself
Which is the punch line

I'm working my magic outside a sad hotel
Signaling to the good strangers of Tallinn

Who know me by my upright faith
And a blind man's stick—snow

In our hair   songs on our lips
Tattered Christ on the telephone line

Stepping out   as they say
Inviolable   tight   alive

And though I don't see it
Lights come on

In the fairy-tale shops
Outside of religion

Or science   who do I think
Is following me?

~

I write: "if I could command you"
Though I don't know who the *you* is

Or the command
No eraser

I fold the page and stick it in my pocket
It was Mary Shelley who said

The beginning is always today
The start   our monster

~

Helsinki   1980
Walking lonesome in the harbor
Spices in the air—
Upriver or down the road
All my friends lived far away
When I think on it now
I'm still twenty-three among Baltic gulls
Humming "My Funny Valentine"
Wind from Estonia blows darkness
Against my cheek
I look warily at strangers
Imagine well of me   I think
Everything will be OK
I wasn't patient yet   or experienced
Why I quoted
Zen and the Art of Motorcycle Maintenance
To a bus driver   I don't remember
Life is on the sides of the mountain and not at the top

Poets in America disappear while still alive
Like birds turned sideways against a hedge
The girl down the street keeps playing
Her violin with the door open
Clouds turn with the wind and
All day a freshness   a sweet smell of dying
Strikes you right in the head   your thinking head
My neighbor   a lepidopterist   finds a tiny black moth
He's never seen before and brings it over
Cupped carefully in his hand

Now he's getting old he wants Bach
A balloon flies over the farm
And he knows this is Bach
Anticipating the enlightenment
He pulls up a blue cornflower
I kick a clod of earth and talk to myself
Poor Bach   He had to dine
With Frederick the Great   who made fun of him
How it is   I think   bending
To pick yet another blazing flower
This is a thing that cannot be done in heaven
Come in   Bach   Over
Tell me of the gallant flourishes
As we leave this life   Over

~

Open your eyes   Close your eyes
It's the same
Low clouds   Winter trees
A girl draws an angel in frost on a windowpane
And why not?   A river
That we call our river
Offers its vow   and why not?
Call me when you get there
The nights get bigger
A neighbor's cat walks the top of our fence
Foolish to speak of the seasons
When we mean *forebears*

~

In memory of Jarkko Laine

I used to go to the botanical gardens in Helsinki
Once   they were owned by the czar of Russia
I'd weep among the flowers

Jarkko   it was fun being poets when we were young
The cold organic smell of cobblestones in rain

> *In the rapt evening that will never be night*
> *you listen without end to Theocritus' nightingale.*
>
> JORGE LUIS BORGES

Frail wisdom

It's your hands I love

Drumming silently

As you count the apples falling

~

The paper wasps flew all afternoon through the ruined woodpile
Some were fast   driven by errands urgent and mysterious
Others circled a log as if their forerunners had once been there

It was risky to get so close when I couldn't see
I sat unmoving beside their stump
Right off   one alighted in my hair
He moved across my scalp like a windblown seed

Because I thought it   he flew

Old baseball glove
Toy of the blind kid
Who sniffed its oiled leather
Who could not use it
Sometimes he'd cry into it

Do you understand that dark joy?

~

In the monastery at Valamo
I took a sauna with a monk
Who was one hundred years old
In the steam his skin smelled
Like strawberries
What do you like to eat? I asked
Strawberries he said

He spends his life
Believing there's another
Standing on his own shoulders
Looking out to sea

∼

I love the horse at Lascaux
So unsecured and fast
Legs vanishing
Even as we look
No one to tame her
Only the river's light

~

Write poems in the mornings
Pour out yesterday's tea
Think of Helen Keller
Who dove into life as
A cormorant hits the sea
The speed of that dive
Me? I entered this world
Already lost   having come
From Mithraic light
Whose sun falls across these pages

TOUCH IT

> *Out there.   The mind of the river
> as it might be you.*
>
> ADRIENNE RICH, "STUDY OF HISTORY"

I fill my bag with apples
To disengage myself
From those corpses of me
—Whitman's phrase—
Then walk uphill
With no plans at all

~

Please Lord don't let me die in this bitterness
Once in Portugal I helped fishermen retrieve their nets
I didn't know them
Please Lord
I wish to hear the surf as I go

For Sophia

I know what they did
To your daughters
Some days I lie in a field
Spreading my arms
Once   years ago   during
A dark winter I tried
In vain to write a poem
In your honor   I was earnest
And the thing turned out
Like a nursery rhyme
But because it was for you
I kept it in a box
There's nothing wrong
With innocence
Though I don't say it
Or I do   but only
In the proper hour
When I'm bowed
By injustice and need
Something like the first flower
I ever brought home
I admit it   I know very little
Rain now
I prefer to think
There's another life to come

∽

Haavikko says—
There is no footpath to the gods

But there's underbrush
I used to lie down

Between moonworts
And one-eyed ferns

༂

Oh the hay-scented fern
Interrupted fern

Royal   sensitive
Ostrich fern   its head in the ground

A note left on Rilke's grave

You saw the sightless men of Paris
Led by crones and children
How you hated them!
You heard them
Speak in a low gibberish
And you shivered
At their cataracts
Here: a blind man's kerchief
Embossed just for you
With Braille   Touch it . . .

∼

When you're blind but can still
See colors   the summer apples

Temper a greenness not of this world
I go about my business

Just another amateur holy man
Meanwhile   reading Orwell:

For whom   for what
Was that bird singing?

No mate   no rival was watching it
What made it sit

At the edge of the lonely wood
And pour its music

Into nothingness?

~

Late afternoon
Railway station
I've got Salvatore Quasimodo
Inside
No one knows . . .

Talking to the blind horse

So much of what I do
Is unimportant

A troll who loves geese
Protects lost animals

Down valley the river
Has melted and frozen again

Reading Nietzsche
At twenty I saw
That his eagles were real
And how little
He loved them
Go ahead
I told myself
Vow to be respectful

Sometimes I feel like Rousseau
Who   exiled from France
Walked the British countryside with his dog   Sultan
Together they smelled the unfamiliar English flowers

~

The branches
Of the yew are fragrant
Small birds I can't identify
Are high in its branches
My heart beats steadily
Why   wrote Ikkyū
Is it all so beautiful this fake dream
This craziness why?
Morning smells of pines
The little dog raises his sweet face my way
Again   I'm a young student translating a poem:
You came close   Hoarfrost   and snow was coming on
Clouds and branches at the windows
All night the stars were like a song
I went in   singing their song   step by step

After reading John Milton I lie down in Sarah
Bernhardt's coffin

You know how it is   late in the day
Milton's angels in your throat

Here comes the delivery van
Sturdy men lugging the thing

My great-grandfather   a wheelwright
Built caskets from stray boards

But hers doubled as a coffee table
With this extra trick

Guests went home   She lay in her casket
Clutching one pink peony

I remember my first undertaker's smile
Churlish   white—flash

Of exceptional teeth—then his lips
Remembered to cover the gravestones

But not before his awkward flex
You can't afford the Conquistador

The casket that conquers death
Sarah   drink your marlish ichor

Milton   *sola fide*   let's play cards

Thinking of Louis Simpson

I was too blind for the army
So I stayed home with a radio

Remember those pressure hoses
In gas stations
That set off chimes
When tires rolled over them?

America   Boy Scouts   flags
And me   sightless

I tried telling you
How I loved your poems
What a veteran presence you had

I was the boy
Who leaned close—
The Zenith hot

Yes   I'm coming to the point

~

The poets always say "if"
As in: if the soul gets loose

Have you seen the black geese
Eating cold rowan berries?
Trust me   the soul has "if-freedoms"

Lately I've been laughing
Like one who's been rowing all day
In an open boat

I like the poets of "if" who are many—
Lucille Clifton: "i rise up above my self / like a fish flying"
Lucie Brock-Broido: "I, abstract, adoring, distant / And unsalvageable"
Marvin Bell: "The 'I' in the poem is not you but someone
who knows a lot about you"
Martín Espada: "The poet's house was a city of glass"

∼

Meanwhile   crossing the street
Shadow vehicles come at me from all directions

If shows off its Kyoto armor
If wants nothing   which makes it
A chess problem for the imagination
If is an amber glow over the village
If will catch you but not today
If says no blank space here
If wants to run you up to the edge of death
If knows full well even the hill's a shadow

When I was very small
My father bought me a kite
You can imagine
That sightless boy
Holding on to a string
Of *his* imaginings

NORDIC ZEN

I always had within me the fear of failing, not in my life, but in my death.

SIMONE WEIL

In Nordic Zen things simply disappear
A man may find he is no longer the emperor of his room
A girl sees at last that her mother doesn't love anybody
A clock chimes at the back of the house

My great-grandfather built
Coffins and sleighs in rural Finland

That they looked alike was no surprise
The rules of construction are the same above and below ground

I drag the old boat to the lakeshore
And talk peaceably to my dead father
About light that shines in the shallows

~

No one calls your name quite like the birches
Which have so many voices
The trick is to hear this and to live at the same time

~

Deep down there's moonlight on the river
We know it's the river we cross again and again
Halfway across   our coins become useless

~

They took us to cemeteries   many times   always in the hot car
And there were oak trees   hyacinths   women's hats
Grandmother spoke words of fright with a Finnish accent
We learned to sit still
Letting sadnesses trail from the windows

It wasn't much
Just a spoon in the dirt
Where the hospital once stood . . .

~

Deep in the night everyone's alive
Even my dark grandmother
In the old café I raise a demitasse with a chipped gold rim

What do the people say in the next village
They're just talking to horses in the winter wind
No hand gestures necessary

∼

Once on a train to Lapland
I loaned my harmonica to a sick man

He played a tune called "There Are No Skunks in Finland"
I wrote that myself he said and coughed up some blood

~

They used to hang the bread from rafters
They had lullabies you wouldn't sing to children nowadays
Their offspring thought nothing of carrying a broken angel across
    the fields . . .

~

Death comes so softly
Like the good man who brings the cattle in . . .

And here we are
Sitting in the woods beside the abandoned woodstove . . .

Yesterday I climbed into a boat
Left to rot on dry land

In among the weathered wood
Souls are talking

HOMINATICUM

*The end is what it is: therefore it is rather foolish to rush.
The book doesn't change.*

PENTTI SAARIKOSKI

As a child I harvested
Black currants with garden shears
Now I see them again
Scissoring among wet leaves
Snow in the branches
What happens
Is more than we can carry
Someone has to sing so I do
Beside the hole   my father's grave

~

Happily sharing our sanity
Is losing a thing together

We didn't know it
A game we played

I enter the woods
The long day runs
Away
We will not meet

People I remember
Up late beside a lamp

In a Lisbon hotel

The wall clock says no one checks out alive
Beneath our window an old-fashioned
Organ-grinder walks in circles
(No truth from either source
Best head to the streets)
I shall lean against a lime tree
Pick my teeth while black gulls
Strut about like James Cagney

Sometimes a poem is a way of
Sitting at the end of a bench
With an imaginary cap over your ears
Which hat will I wear this winter?
I'm the king of the unswerving
Watch as I whittle this stick

Big poem mates with little poem:
They produce an essay
A child hidden subsequently
In an Irish laundry

The academy fears deformed children

~

I watch you sewing
I study your method
Your formula is based on a map of the stars
I use the seahorse's coordinates

～

You touch my hair
Saying   great crested grebe

Among reeds
A floating nest

~

Cold river of childhood
A boat ride in Finland
A girl with golden hair
Played a flute
Something . . . something . . .
It's winter in this life
There's nothing to do
This much I know:
Night doesn't push us
But the days . . .

Growing old talking to myself
Reaching for chestnuts

~

Meanwhile
Catbirds drift me

Under yellow leaves
Among birches

Since wandering blind
Isn't straight

A dear child has many names
Finnish proverb   Dear child
Buttercup   Mockingbird
Mouse behind the chanterelle
So what that the clouds are low?

∼

I am
In me is this eye   this stream   this wind
This murmuration of birds in flight

I am present tense
Forever

In you I am a green song

~

Some children knew the names of birds
My favorite was the white-throated sparrow
Whom we called the Peabody bird
His song could break your heart
The wood thrush was also a heartbreaker
Lying face down in the woods he'd get inside you
He'd get inside because I was playing dead
This was in the final days before television
We played dead and listened to birds

~

When spirits come in the forest
Something happens first
It gets quiet . . .
This is your moment to run
If you still have the legs underneath you
Otherwise the assumption is you're in.

Perhaps misremembered from Martin Shaw

∼

You bend to the pavement
Pick up pennies
Write your name
On park benches
Or better yet
Someone else's name
In general it's a good day
When they don't call you
A monster or a friend of one

~

Seeing I was blind and on vacation
A man climbed a palm tree
And brought me a coconut
Handing it over
He warned me to beware
Of the devil—do you
Understand? People
The world over
Think the blind are possessed
I'm guessing this
Doesn't happen to you

~

I dreamed last night of a friend whom I insulted
Almost twenty years ago
We haven't spoken since
He was trying to sell me a shirt
That's how the unconscious works
There's plenty of suppressed rage
In the haberdashery

∼

In another dream
At one point I was wearing a turtle shell
Preparing to advertise underwear
On a Manhattan street
I was worried about my guide dog
Who would look after her
While I wandered   disguised as a turtle
A charming policeman of the unconscious
Said he'd look after my dog
I began crying because he led my dog away
I mean   how do you get out of a turtle suit
And get your dog back in the city of the Id

∼

Winter with a book
Alone with old-man teeth   What a thing!
Steam from the lake   What a thing!
Drumroll   Shostakovich
Train whistle
Dog barking far off
Hot tea
Fireside
Odysseus sailing . . .

Now that the wind has stopped
Now when I look at the sails
And take stock of my journey
I see the stars and the ocean
Are closer together

~

One makes the world while drinking tea
Another while running for his life

No matter   the old soupy mind
Runs cold   This is something

To love

∼

And slow life is the work
We turn to good
So we think

Let us be slow
Let us be very slow

EMPTY PLACES

The world
There are many collapsed histories,
many ink-stained explanations of why.

ARTO MELLERI

~

Every morning the wisdom of trees
And the blind man who touches them
Didn't you know about the book of the pine?
The ministerial book of the birch
A favorite page that's on the willow just down the hill
Planted long ago   forgotten   untended
Its Lucretian bark tells a hundred stories:
The day we disappeared
The day we came back
The wind that passed three days ago
So many tales of atoms and tears
And flowers standing open beside graves
And here at the base of the tree
Beside the mushrooms   Lucretius himself:
Man's greatest wealth is to live on
A little with contented mind
For little is never lacking

It's raining
And the boy leaves for school

Knowing how the words *no one*
Are a cage that never held a bird

Like the one in his grandmother's attic
What a lovely jagged thing   the rain

For R.S.

In the airport where women and men
Are strangely themselves
As children are in churches
You see how lonely you are
Though you're married
Have children   friends
A loving partner
And laughter
There it is   beside
The vending machines
Your shadow solitude
Searching its pockets
For the right coins
Known also to Caesar

~

They set the boy
Upright   small
In shirtsleeves

In a cold region
Of figures—
Legions

Of scrawls
Scattered
Like dead men

Chalkboard
Battlefield
Child with telescope

He's inside my coat
Morning sun
And walking by the sea

When no one is out

Oh Hush Puppies

I recall that after I wore you for a day or two my father said
Your shoes smell like dead rats
How do you know what dead rats smell like? I asked him
I was in World War II he said

                    ∾

Someone once said *Resolve to be tender with the young*
Compassionate with the aged   sympathetic with the striving
And tolerant with the weak and wrong
Sometime in your life you will have been all of these

Oh Wallace Stevens

You are the blind man's imagined peacock
And by God I heard a real one once
It sounded like a human baby being torn apart
Though I cannot confirm this was its sentiment

∼

Oh Muriel Rukeyser

I love you

You pulled from ether
Penelope's unraveled loomings
And you were funny
God yes

~

Oh Auden

Oh Ted Berrigan

Oh Alice Notley

Oh Herkimer Puccini

My father's nickname for me   growing up

Oh Pentti

> *Elämä on ihmiselle annettu*
> *Jotta hän tarkoin harkitsisi*
> *Missä asennossa tahtoo olla kuollut...*

The rich have "panic rooms" which are like bank vaults
They go right in like Hitler to his bunker
The poor have "panic shoes" which are like
Those puffy red envelopes from bill collectors

Life was given to man
So he might consider
What position he'll assume when dead...

Oh Caruso

He took his mother's hand once
The day his infant sister died
Just the two of them on the steps
Of the church of Gesù Nuovo
They stood and looked across the piazza
At the orange and yellow houses
So cheerful   the sky so impossibly clear
He thought there could be no limbo
No way station for the souls of innocent children
His mother removed her hand from his   whispering
You are too warm

∾

All subsequent tenors want to be him
His was a voice of power   of delicacy
Of warmth and mystery
It's the mystery everyone else lacks

∾

I open old books to see if postcards fall out

I'm reading the youthful notebooks
Of a long-dead Finnish commie poet
And it's raining in my neighborhood

I too desire houses for the poor and a horse for each child

Meantime I think of Saint Francis of Assisi   his death
What it means to poetry

~

I love it whenever the poets say angels visit them
I like untruths as much as I like stars and lingonberries

Remember when you were a kid and had lots of green clothes?

A poem a day   sometimes two
A neighbor's parakeet
Books pulled at random from their shelves
No one is in charge
Least of all the locksmith
I do not know my maker
My voice is a mystery

This life is a shipboard affair—
Radio signals come:
Turn eighty degrees starboard
Reduce speed
At this longitude
I own a notebook
Of mid-ocean static
And all I'm doing
Is simply crossing a room

∼

Coffee late morning
A few poems by a friend
Unwearied the coo and choke of doves
I will make a joy of it

Light from the cold branches
Carrying words of others
I will make a joy of it

ABOUT THE AUTHOR

Stephen Kuusisto teaches at Syracuse University. His books include the poetry collections *Only Bread, Only Light, Letters to Borges,* and *Old Horse, What Is to Be Done?* as well as the memoirs *Planet of the Blind, Eavesdropping,* and *Have Dog, Will Travel: A Poet's Journey.* Visit his website at www.stephenkuusisto.com.

Poets for Poetry

Copper Canyon Press poets are at the center of all our efforts as a nonprofit publisher. Poets not only create the art that defines our books, but they read and teach the books we publish. Many are also generous donors who believe in financially supporting the larger poetry community of Copper Canyon Press. For decades, our poets have quietly donated their royalties, have directly engaged in our fundraising campaigns, and have made personal donations in support of the next generation. Their support has encouraged the innovative risk-taking that sustains and furthers the art form.

The donor-poets who have contributed to the Press since 2023 include:

Jonathan Aaron
Kelli Russell Agodon
Pamela Alexander
Joyce Harrington Bahle
Ellen Bass
Mark Bibbins
Sherwin Bitsui
Marianne Boruch
Laure-Anne Bosselaar
Cyrus Cassells
Peter Cole and Adina Hoffman
Elizabeth J. Coleman
John Freeman
Forrest Gander
Jenny George
Daniel Gerber
Julian Gewirtz
Jorie Graham
Robert and Carolyn Hedin
Bob Hicok
Ha Jin
Jaan Kaplinski
Laura Kasischke
Jennifer L. Knox
Ted Kooser
Deborah Landau
Sung-Il Lee
Ben Lerner
Dana Levin
Heather McHugh
Jane Miller
Lisa Olstein
Gregory Orr
Eric Pankey
Kevin Prufer
Paisley Rekdal
James Richardson
Alberto Ríos
David Romtvedt
Natalie Shapero
Arthur Sze
Elaine Terranova
Chase Twichell
Ocean Vuong
Connie Wanek-Dentinger
Emily Warn

Poetry is vital to language and living. Since 1972, Copper Canyon Press has published extraordinary poetry from around the world to engage the imaginations and intellects of readers, writers, booksellers, librarians, teachers, students, and donors.

WE ARE GRATEFUL FOR THE MAJOR SUPPORT PROVIDED BY:

THE PAUL G. ALLEN FAMILY FOUNDATION

> TO LEARN MORE ABOUT UNDERWRITING
> COPPER CANYON PRESS TITLES,
> PLEASE CALL 360-385-4925 EXT. 105

WE ARE GRATEFUL FOR THE MAJOR SUPPORT PROVIDED BY:

Anonymous

Jill Baker and Jeffrey Bishop

Anne and Geoffrey Barker

Donna Bellew

Lisha Bian

Will Blythe

John Branch

Diana Broze

John R. Cahill

Sarah J. Cavanaugh

Keith Cowan and Linda Walsh

Peter Currie

Geralyn White Dreyfous

The Evans Family

Mimi Gardner Gates

Gull Industries Inc.
    on behalf of William True

Carolyn and Robert Hedin

David and Jane Hibbard

Bruce S. Kahn

Phil Kovacevich and Eric Wechsler

Maureen Lee and Mark Busto

Ellie Mathews and Carl Youngmann
    as The North Press

Larry Mawby and Lois Bahle

Petunia Charitable Fund and
    adviser Elizabeth Hebert

Suzanne Rapp and Mark Hamilton

Adam and Lynn Rauch

Emily and Dan Raymond

Joseph C. Roberts

Cynthia Sears

Kim and Jeff Seely

Tree Swenson

Julia Sze

Barbara and Charles Wright

In honor of C.D. Wright
    from Forrest Gander

Caleb Young as C. Young Creative

The dedicated interns and faithful
    volunteers of Copper Canyon Press

The pressmark for Copper Canyon Press
suggests entrance, connection, and interaction
while holding at its center
an attentive, dynamic space for poetry.

This book is set in Calluna.
Book design by Phil Kovacevich.

www.ingramcontent.com/pod-product-compliance
Lightning Source LLC
Jackson TN
JSHW082337270525
85144JS00015B/218